IT'S TIME TO EAT GREEN BEANS

It's Time to Eat Green Beans

Walter the Educator

Silent King Books
A WhichHead Entertainment Imprint

Copyright © 2024 by Walter the Educator

All rights reserved. No part of this book may be reproduced in any manner whatsoever without written per- mission except in the case of brief quotations embodied in critical articles and reviews.

First Printing, 2024

Disclaimer

This book is a literary work; the story is not about specific persons, locations, situations, and/or circumstances unless mentioned in a historical context. Any resemblance to real persons, locations, situations, and/or circumstances is coincidental. This book is for entertainment and informational purposes only. The author and publisher offer this information without warranties expressed or implied. No matter the grounds, neither the author nor the publisher will be accountable for any losses, injuries, or other damages caused by the reader's use of this book. The use of this book acknowledges an understanding and acceptance of this disclaimer.

It's Time to Eat Green Beans is a collectible early learning book by Walter the Educator suitable for all ages belonging to Walter the Educator's Time to Eat Book Series. Collect more books at WaltertheEducator.com

USE THE EXTRA SPACE TO TAKE NOTES AND DOCUMENT YOUR MEMORIES

GREEN BEANS

It's time to eat, come take a seat,

It's Time to Eat

Green Beans

A special veggie we'll soon meet.

Long and slender, green and bright,

Green beans make a yummy bite!

Look at them lined up in a row,

Little beans that start to grow.

They grew on vines with sun above,

Now they're here, ready to love!

Green beans tall, green beans lean,

So crisp, so fresh, so bright and clean.

They snap when bent, a little crunch,

Perfect for a tasty lunch!

Take a nibble, take a bite,

Green beans give us pure delight.

They're mild and sweet, so smooth and neat,

A healthy snack that's hard to beat!

It's Time to Eat Green Beans

Inside each bean, so snug and tight,

Are tiny seeds, tucked out of sight.

They hold the power to make you strong,

Helping you all day long!

In salads cool, or soups so warm,

Green beans come in every form.

Cooked or raw, they taste just right,

On every plate, a welcome sight.

Pile them high, or keep them low,

Watch them roll and bounce just so!

With little bites, or big ones too,

Green beans are good for me and you.

Sometimes long, and sometimes short,

Green beans come in every sort.

A skinny shape that's fun to see,

Perfect for you, perfect for me.

Take your fork, or use your hands,

Eating green beans is so grand!

They help you grow, they help you run,

It's Time to Eat
Green
Beans

Green beans make eating fun!

So next time beans are on your plate,

Pick them up, don't make them wait!

Munch them down, then feel the power,

Green beans help you every hour.

ABOUT THE CREATOR

Walter the Educator is one of the pseudonyms for Walter Anderson. Formally educated in Chemistry, Business, and Education, he is an educator, an author, a diverse entrepreneur, and he is the son of a disabled war veteran. "Walter the Educator" shares his time between educating and creating. He holds interests and owns several creative projects that entertain, enlighten, enhance, and educate, hoping to inspire and motivate you. Follow, find new works, and stay up to date with Walter the Educator™

at WaltertheEducator.com

www.ingramcontent.com/pod-product-compliance
Lightning Source LLC
LaVergne TN
LVHW052012060526
838201LV00059B/3993